D1204156

**Stamp Collecting**

PROPERTY OF LAURIE COHOON
CHRISTMAS, 1972
FROM MOM & DAD

Illustrated Teach Yourself

designer
Gerald Wilkinson

KENYA, UGANDA
AND TANGANYIKA

1938 – 1954

Wmk Multipl
Script CA
Various
perforatio

L. N. and M. Williams

Illustrated Teach Yourself **Stamp Collecting**

 **Brockhampton Press**

ISBN 0 340 14951 5
This edition first published 1972
Copyright © 1972 L N & M Williams

All rights reserved. No part of this publication may be
reproduced or transmitted in any form or by any means,
electronic or mechanical, including photocopy, recording,
or any information storage and retrieval system, without
permission in writing from the publisher, Brockhampton
Press Ltd, Salisbury Road, Leicester, LEI 7QS
Printed in Great Britain by Fletcher & Son Ltd, Norwich

Except where specifically noted otherwise,
all stamps illustrated in this book are
enlarged $1\frac{1}{2}$ times.

Contents

The boy
stood on

the burning

deck

# 1  *The interest in stamps*

*The boy stood on the burning deck...*
   'What has that to do with stamp collecting?'
   'Nothing ——'
   'Then why begin that way in a book about stamps?'
   'Let me finish the sentence, please. As I was about to say: nothing, nothing you can think of is entirely unconnected with stamps or their designs if you look for the connection. Take the boy on the burning deck. Boys are shown on many stamps. Several are playing cricket on the 2½ + 1 cent of New Zealand's 1969 Health issue, and others appear on earlier stamps of that country and other countries. Burning fires can be seen on the 1d of St Helena of 1967 marking the 300 years of settlement since the Great Fire of London. Another fire stamp came from Canada in 1956 as publicity for Fire Prevention Week. The deck, of course, was part of the ship, and there are so many ships on stamps that to refer to every one of them would occupy a book larger than this. In 1969 Great Britain issued a series of six ship stamps. Among them were the QE2 and some famous old-time sailing ships, such as the *Cutty Sark* and the *Great Britain*.'

   That conversation merely illustrates what an enormous range of interest is presented by designs on stamps. Many collectors still fill their albums along conventional lines by arranging the stamps by country, date of issue and values, but others prefer to collect by designs alone and form thematic, or topical, collections.
   Themes and subjects for such collections are almost endless. Among the most popular

topics are sport, space travel, aircraft, ships and architecture.

**Sport**

Sport offers a huge variety. Olympic Games stamps alone can provide enough material to fill several albums. As the Games are held at four-yearly intervals the number of stamps keeps increasing. Nowadays many countries issue stamps commemorating the Games even though the issuing nations do not take part in any event. Among those which did compete in the 1968 Games in Mexico, Czechoslovakia, Belgium, Germany, Poland and of course Mexico itself, to mention only a few, all issued special commemorative series. The Czechoslovakian set shows not only contestants but also ancient Aztec figures and designs from Mexican history.

Sports stamps and sporting stamps have been issued on many other occasions also. Several parts of the British Commonwealth have made issues featuring cricket. To celebrate the MCC

tour of the West Indies in 1968 Guyana and Jamaica each issued three stamps, and Barbados included a splendid action picture of Gary Sobers in an Independence set in 1966.

Football is extensively represented, and sets commemorating World Cup contests have come from Great Britain, many Commonwealth countries, France, Germany, Sweden, Israel and others. In 1966 Great Britain brought out a special 4d stamp to celebrate England's victory in the Cup.

Some unusual sports can be seen on stamps. Pelota is the subject of the design of a French 40 francs stamp in 1956. Lacrosse is shown on a special 5 cents stamp issued by Canada in 1968.

**Space travel**

When Yuri Gagarin became the first cosmonaut to travel in space in 1961, his native country the USSR issued three stamps to celebrate that outstanding event, and its date, 12—IV—1961, is incorporated in the designs. His portrait is shown on the 3 kopeck and 10 kopeck stamps. Since then the same country has issued other space flight stamps, such as the two which appeared in August 1961 in honour of Titov's flight. Space probes and associated subjects are shown on the stamps of a number of countries, and Czechoslovakia has issued many such stamps.

The United States of America has issued several stamps to commemorate space achievements. A 10 cents was issued to celebrate the great landmark in history, the first man on the moon in July 1969. A curious thing about that stamp is that the figures of value make it seem that it was Apollo 10 which landed on the moon; that is just a freak of the design, and Apollo 11 was responsible. The first USA space stamp was a 4 cents in 1962 for 'Project Mercury', when Colonel John Glenn became the first American to travel in space. Two 5 cents stamps printed se-tenant (joined together) came in September 1967, showing Gemini IV above the earth and an astronaut walking in space.

Those very few examples of space flight stamps indicate what a large field of collecting interest lies in that topic. If not only the stamps but envelopes and cards with special postmarks are added to the collection it can become really sizeable.

Yuri Gagarin on a space
stamp from Czechoslovakia

Rockets and sputniks
leaving earth, on a Czech
50h stamp of 1963

U.S.A. 1970 (enlarged x 2½)

**Stamps on stamps**

A topic which has attracted many collectors is that of stamps on stamps. In 1840 Great Britain issued the world's first postage stamps because of postal reforms brought about by Sir Rowland Hill. Other countries followed the lead in the next few years. Issues commemorating the hundredth anniversary of early stamps are numerous. Most of them reproduce the original designs. As the early stamps are, generally speaking, rather rare and expensive, the reproduced forms appearing on the centenary stamps enable the original early stamps to be cheaply represented in a collection. That is not to suggest that any reproduction is as good as an original, and pictures of stamps do not belong to a collection, but where the reproduction is part of the design of an actual postage stamp it is a perfectly collectable item.

Great Britain 1840
Penny Black with red
Maltese cross postmark

Stamp Centenary issue
of Great Britain 1940

Great Britain's centenary issue in 1940 showed the head of Queen Victoria as it appeared on the 'Penny Black' of 1840, and also the head of King George VI. In 1970, to commemorate the Philympia stamp exhibition, Britain issued a set reproducing 3 early stamps, among them the 'Penny Black'. France in 1949 issued 15 and 25 francs stamps in the same design as that used in 1849. The first German state to issue postage stamps was Bavaria, also in 1849, but it ceased to have its own stamps in 1920, so to mark the centenary the German Federal Republic issued three stamps showing the centenarians. Because the old currency, kreuzer, had gone out of use many years earlier the German stamps bore values of 10, 20 and 30 pfennig instead of 1, 3 and 6 kreuzer. More recently, in 1969, two stamps from Gambia pictured its stamps issued a hundred years before.

First Gambian stamp shown on centenary issue of 1969

**The Arts**

Literature is very plentifully represented on stamps. For the 400th anniversary of William Shakespeare's birth Great Britain issued five stamps in 1964. Four of them showed his portrait, and all five depict characters from his plays. Goethe and Schiller have appeared on stamps of their native Germany, Dante on issues from Italy and other countries such as Malta in 1965. Victor Hugo, François Rabelais and Jules Verne can all be seen on issues of France.

Below: Shakespeare commemorative, Great Britain 1964 and a French stamp of 1955 showing Jules Verne and the *Nautilus* from *20,000 Leagues Under the Sea*

Johann Sebastian Bach on a
German stamp of 1961

Music on stamps forms a specially large group. Rossini appears on an Italian series of 1942. Dvořák is to be seen on Czechoslovakian 50 haleru of 1934. In 1969 Austria issued a souvenir sheet of nine stamps showing scenes from operas performed at the Vienna State Opera House.

Do your interests lie in history? Stamps themselves by their very issue reflect part of the history of the issuing countries, but many of them have issued stamps with historical subjects. Several English kings and queens can be seen on stamps of Great Britain and the Commonwealth. Queen Elizabeth I is portrayed on the British 4d of 1968. Three kings of England and a queen surround the head of King George VI on New Zealand's 1½d stamp of 1940. James I is shown on Newfoundland's 1 cent of 1910.

The history of the American War of Independence is well illustrated on issues of USA from 1925 onwards, and the American Civil War is commemorated on two 4 cents and three 5 cents appearing between 1961 and 1965.

Those are only a few examples, and they merely hint at the vast range of interest presented by stamp designs. Forming a thematic, topical or subject collection is indeed simply a matter of choosing your subject and getting started.

Stamp collecting is a grand hobby. If you have only just taken up collecting, or are thinking about beginning now, you may wonder what attractions there can be in these scraps of coloured paper, for some specimens of which people have been known to search for almost a lifetime and pay fabulous sums of money. It is not easy to explain in words the magic influence which stamps exert over millions of collectors throughout the world. When you have been collecting for some time,

American Civil War battles
commemorative, 1965

Queen Elizabeth I on Great Britain stamp of 1968

Five English sovereigns on New Zealand issue, 1940

Prince of Wales investiture commemorative, 1969

and if you study your stamps carefully, you yourself will experience that mystic 'urge' to become a full-blooded philatelist.

Philately is the technical term by which stamp collecting is generally known. The word was coined during the eighteen-sixties by a French collector, M. Georges Herpin, who based it on the Greek *philos* (love of) and *ateleia* (that which exempts from tax). If a letter has had the postage prepaid on it by means of stamps, no further tax is payable. Philatelists are people who follow philately, which is understood to mean the study of stamps rather than simply their collection.

**Extra interest** Apart from their designs, stamps are far more interesting than you might think when you glance at them for the first time. There are sure to be fascinating stories about the way in which the issues were planned, how the designs were chosen, the method of printing, the kind of paper and watermark used, and many other details which you will want to discover if you become a philatelist. In other chapters you will be able to read how to distinguish between the different varieties of printing, paper, watermark and perforation.

Although it is usually not very difficult to discover the details of modern stamps, it is much harder to have to piece together the stories of early issues which appeared perhaps fifty or a hundred years before you were born; but that has been done, and it is the most fascinating side of philately. Of course, a great deal is known and has been recorded about the old stamps, and this knowledge forms the basis on which later studies can be founded; but it is really thrilling, once you have begun to study your stamps properly, to make new discoveries about which earlier collectors knew nothing, and sometimes you may be able to form new theories which contradict what has been written before. By the time you can do that you will have become an important philatelist, and will have realized what a wonderfully interesting subject philately is.

## 2 *Forming a general collection*

When you begin to collect stamps, it will be best if you take them from all over the world, and do not confine your collection to the issues of one group, such as the British Commonwealth or a single country.

The more stamps you see, and handle, in your early days as a collector, the more will your philatelic knowledge grow, and this knowledge will prove helpful to you later on, particularly if you decide to specialize. Of course, even if you do collect the world's stamps, it does not mean to say that you can expect to form a complete collection or even obtain at least one specimen from every country, although that is quite a good target at which to aim.

If you have only a few stamps to start with, your best course will be to buy a packet, as large as you can afford, from a dealer. Packets of many kinds and sizes are obtainable but be sure to ask for one in which the stamps are all different, otherwise you will be getting duplicates which, although perhaps of some use for exchanging, will not be needed in your collection.

At the same time you will need an album. If you have received one as a present you will not have any choice as to its size or scope; but if you have to buy one you should make your selection carefully. There is a wide range of albums, some with printed spaces for stamps, others with blank pages, some fast bound, and others with binders which allow the leaves to be removed and rearranged. In the beginning do not be too ambitious in your choice. It may seem very fine to go home with a large album capable of holding 50,000 stamps or more tucked proudly under your arm; but when you have mounted all your stamps and find that they occupy only a few isolated pages, and after you have spent months trying vainly to fill the blanks, much of the pleasure will have gone, and you will be inclined to give up in despair.

It is far better to begin modestly with a small album costing less than £1 or so. Not only will your collection show up to much more advantage in those surroundings, but any mistakes you make (and you are sure to make some at first — everybody does) will not be so serious.

Your first album can be of the fast-bound kind. Each page should have the country name and a few illustrations at the top. The rest of the page may be blank with outlines for stamps, or with an all-over pattern of small squares, called *quadrillé*. This is by far the best type for a beginner. Choose an album with pages as thick as you can get them; they will be less likely to tear when you remove a stamp from one position to another. When you buy your album, ask for a few dozen sheets of transparent interleaving paper of the same size. This paper is very necessary to put between opposite pages rather heavily laden with stamps, as it prevents them from rubbing against each other and perhaps becoming creased or torn.

Having brought your album home, look through the pages, make a mental note of the names of the countries, and become familiar with the designs of stamps illustrated. When you have done that, get out your stamps and spread them, face upwards, on the table in front of you.

Your first task will be to sort them into countries, in other words, to identify each specimen. This is not as easy as it sounds.

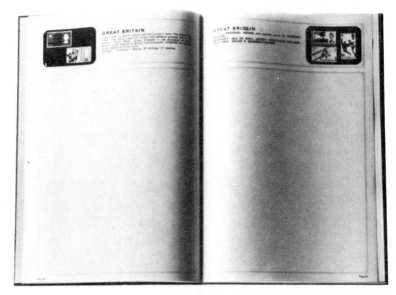

One of Stanley Gibbons's small fast-bound albums

A Bulgarian stamp inscribed in Cyrillic letters

Many foreign countries do not spell their names in the same way as we do, and some even use different alphabets, so that until you become experienced you will have to proceed step by step. It is impossible here to give you hints on how to identify every stamp you are likely to come across, but there are several identification charts which you can buy quite cheaply and which will help you with a large number of stamps. To begin with, here are hints on recognizing some of the more difficult specimens.

Among the European nations Russia, Bulgaria and Greece use alphabets different from our own. The Russian and Bulgarian alphabets, known as Cyrillic, are the same, and can be recognized, because they include a reversed R, a B without the upper loop and a V upside down. Most modern Russian stamps contain the letters CCCP somewhere in the design (the initials in Russian of the Union of Soviet Socialist Republics). If you have a stamp you cannot identify which is inscribed in the Cyrillic alphabet and does not bear those initials, it might be an older Russian issue,

Russia

Greece

Hungary

Turkey

East Germany

Albania

Japan

China

joslavia

vitzerland

orway

used in the times of the Czars, but it may be Bulgarian. Compare it with the Russian and Bulgarian stamps illustrated, and see whether you can find any points of similarity. Yugoslavians use the same alphabet, but most of their stamps, except the early ones, are inscribed also with the name of the country in Roman letters. The 'Chainbreakers' stamp illustrated is a typical early issue and may help you to recognize other Yugoslavians.

Greek is similar to the Cyrillic alphabet, but many of the letters are squarer, and nearly all Greek stamps are inscribed *ΕΛΛΑΣ*. Modern Turkish issues contain the word 'Türkiye'.

Switzerland nowadays inscribes her stamps with 'Helvetia' (Switzerland in Latin), West Germany is 'Deutsche Bundespost', East Germany is 'DDR' or 'Deutsche Demokratische Republik', Albania is 'Shqipni', 'Shqiptare' or 'Shqipënia', and Austria is 'Österreich'; but some early Austrian newspaper stamps have no country inscriptions at all. Hungary is 'Magyar' and Norway is 'Norge' or 'Noreg'; but you should not have much difficulty with other European issues.

Probably your greatest problems will arise when you come to identify Asiatic stamps. Among the most difficult will be some issues of the Indian Native States, China and Japan. On stamps of Japan watch for the square-looking character with a line through the centre. Some Chinese stamps are inscribed with the name of the country in English, but others can usually be recognized by the rather square-looking characters with tails.

Stamps of the Indian Native States are more of a problem, and some, such as issues of Jammu and Kashmir, Alwar, Faridkot and a few others, do not bear any English characters at all. The same applies to stamps of Saudi-Arabia. You will find it best to examine the pictures of stamps from Alwar, Bahawalpur,

22

Saudi-Arabian issue
(Hejaz-Nejd)

Bundi and Hyderabad, so as to become
familiar with the type of inscriptions to be
found on these issues. There is also an
illustration of a Saudi-Arabian stamp.
Other countries whose stamps might puzzle
you are Manchuria, Mongolia and Siam (or
Thailand), but the pictures should help you in
identification if you look carefully at the native
inscriptions and compare them with those on
your specimens. It is as well to remember that
the characters may not be exactly the same,
but a few of them may be so similar that you
will be able to recognize them without much
difficulty.

Thailand

Indian Native State (Alwar)

Austrian newspaper
stamp

After sorting your stamps, you will want to examine them to see whether they need cleaning. Specimens with parts of old envelopes or other paper still sticking to their backs should be put on one side for treatment.

Many stamps, especially those printed from engraved recesses (about which you can read in a later chapter), can safely be put into water. Others printed in fugitive colours or on some types of paper will be ruined if they are even damped. Until you know which are which you had better treat all stamps as though they were in fugitive colours, even if it does mean taking more time over them.

You will need a clean shallow dish or a plate into which a little clean water has been put. Then take a piece of clean white blotting-paper about the same size as the dish, and put it in so that it soaks up the water; but see that the paper does not become really very wet, otherwise you have used too much water. When the blotting-paper is damp, put your stamps face upwards on it, taking care that no water reaches their faces. Leave them there for 20—30 minutes, and when you remove the stamps, the paper on their backs should peel off quite easily.

To dry the stamps, lay them out face downwards on a sheet of dry, clean, white blotting-paper, and leave them for about half an hour. If they have curled, when they are quite dry place them between the pages of a book, taking care not to allow any corners to become creased. The stamps will become flat after a few hours, and can then be mounted in your album.

When you have gained experience and know which stamps may be soaked with safety, you can reduce the time taken to prepare your stamps by immersing them in a dish of clean, warm water. The paper on their backs should be released after a few minutes.

This treatment can be applied only to used stamps, and unused specimens with gum should never be allowed to come into contact with water, even if part of the gum has paper sticking to it. A stamp with only part of its original gum is more desirable, and valuable, than one without gum at all.

**Mounting stamps**

Mounting stamps in an album is quite simple if you set about it in the right way. Never use gum or paste to fix the stamps to the pages, and on no account stick unused stamps down with their own gum. If you do so you will ruin not only your album but the stamps as well. Mounting should be done only with specially prepared hinges, small rectangles of transparent paper gummed on one side, which you can buy cheaply from any stamp dealer. Do not try to economize by using adhesive tape, music tape or stamp edging; they will spoil your stamps and album almost as surely as gum.

In order to mount a stamp, hold it face downwards in your left hand with the top of the stamp facing towards your right. Take a mount, gummed side downwards, in your right hand, and very slightly moisten one of the narrow ends, about one-third of the way along. Put the moistened part on the back of the stamp near the top, so that about two-thirds of the mount projects over the edge, and press the stamp and mount carefully together. Then fold the mount backwards, so that the gummed side comes outwards, and press down so that the fold in the mount almost comes level with the top of the stamp, but just does not project over the edge. Next, dab the little finger of your right hand lightly on your tongue and put the finger in the centre of the gummed part of the mount to moisten it. Then turn the stamp over and put it, face upwards, in the position required in your album, pressing down the moistened centre of the mount. The stamp will

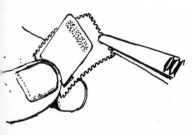

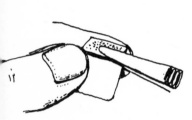

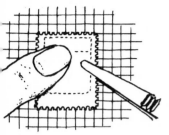

then be firmly in place and you will be able to lift it up, as on a hinge, to examine the back if necessary. Also, if you want to remove the stamp, it will come away cleanly from the page; but do not try to remove any specimen within half an hour of having mounted it, for the gum must dry first.

Some people like never to use a hinge on a mint stamp because, once it has had a hinge affixed, the stamp cannot be described as 'unhinged mint' or 'unmounted mint'. They put each stamp in a plastic strip and affix that to the page. One of the disadvantages of plastic strips (apart from their cost) is that they do not hold stamps in place as securely as hinges do, and the appearance of a page is spoilt when the stamps become displaced in the strips. Most collectors consider a lightly hinged stamp to be as desirable as one that is unhinged mint, but enhanced prices are charged for unhinged stamps.

Whenever you handle or mount stamps, be quite sure that your hands are perfectly clean and dry. Any dirt or moisture on them will be transferred to the stamps, much to their detriment. It is far better to do all 'handling' with a pair of tweezers, which you can obtain from a stamp dealer, and with a little practice you will be able to use them instead of your fingers when sorting and mounting.

# 3 *Errors and varieties*

All stamp collectors are interested in errors and varieties — but, what is an error, and what is a variety?

It is difficult to give exact answers to those questions. Before even trying to do so you must be able to answer another question. What is a normal stamp?

A normal stamp is one that *was* issued in the state in which it was *intended to be issued* by the government or other authority that issued it — perfectly printed, in the intended colours, on the intended paper, with perforations (if any) as intended. . . . The list of things that could have been intended for stamps would be a very long one indeed, but the few that have been mentioned give the general idea of what a normal stamp is.

An error is a mistake, for example a wrong colour because the colour used was not the intended colour, wrong paper, wrong method of perforation, wrong overprint, wrong value, a centre upside down in relation to the frame (inverted centre), and so on through the list of things that were intended for the stamps.

Notice that the design is not mentioned. There is a good reason for leaving it out. Mistakes have been made in designs, and such mistakes are errors, but they form a special class which is called 'artist's errors' or 'errors of design'. They are popular with collectors but are not errors in the philatelic sense, and some of these mistakes are referred to in Chapter 8. Although the issuing authority would not really have wanted a mistake to be made in the design, it was approved for issue. Therefore no stamp with the artist's error is

Peru 1868 1 dinero
with embossed arms
inverted

other than a normal stamp merely because of the artist's error.

**Varieties**   A variety is a stamp with a difference. Sometimes the word 'variety' is used as just another word for stamp. You might say, for example, 'a thousand varieties', meaning no more than 'a thousand different stamps', and in that sense 'variety' does not mean anything different from a normal stamp. It means that the stamps are different from one another.

Because varieties are stamps with differences when compared with normal stamps, errors are varieties. Every error is a variety, but not every variety is an error. What sorts of differences, then, are they that make varieties? They are the differences which occur because of something happening during the stamps' production.

An issuing authority always has the intention that every stamp of the same design should be as alike as possible to every other stamp of the same design because in a sense stamps are money, like government securities. If genuine stamps of the same design varied greatly among themselves there would always be the chance that quite crude forgeries could be used to defraud the issuing authority. But nothing is perfect, and minute differences do occur — they cannot be prevented — and stamps which the authority would really like to be identical do have differences. So, instead of insisting that every stamp, so to speak, scores 10 out of 10, the issuing authority allows stamps which score 9 out of 10 to be issued. Anything with less than 10 out of 10 is a variety.

Not all varieties are important. An important variety is one that tells part of the story of how the *stamps* were produced. An unimportant variety is one that tells no more than that something went amiss when *that particular stamp* was produced. Some important varieties have only minute differences from the

Cook Islands 1967 4c wrongly inscribed 'Walter Lily' instead of 'Water Lily'

Austria 1934 6 groschen with man's ears reversed

Austria 1935 6 groschen with ears corrected

An error of colour: Western Australia 1879 2d printed mauve instead of yellow

normal stamps. By contrast, some varieties that have striking differences are quite unimportant – like gaps appearing between differently coloured portions of a stamp printed in several colours.

Can you tell, by looking at a variety, whether it is important or unimportant? Yes and no. Some varieties are obvious, others are very difficult, and it takes years of experience to be certain in some cases.

To understand how errors and varieties occur you must have some knowledge of stamp production. It is very complicated, and has many different stages. To give a bird's-eye view you could say that someone must

Examples of inverted
overprints : above, Togo (actual size)
below : Greece

Austrian stamp with inverted centre

prepare the design and decide on the shape and colours. Someone else must provide the paper and decide whether it is to have a watermark and be gummed. Someone else must prepare all the necessary things for the printing – and these preparations have many complications which are different for different printing methods, of which there are many. Then the stamps have to be printed and, probably, perforated. Then checked.

All the errors that delight collectors have come into their hands because the errors escaped the vigilance of the checkers whose job it is to see that mistakes do not pass out of the printing works.

# 4 *Printing*

Four main methods are used in stamp printing. Printers know them by different names, but collectors often call them recess printing (line-engraving), photogravure, typography (or surface printing) and lithography.

Line-engraving was employed for the first stamps in 1840, and has been used for many issues since then, including the current high values of Great Britain. The first stage in this process is the preparation of a drawing, often in water-colours, from which the engraver is to work. The engraver, a highly skilled craftsman, cuts the design in reverse into a small block of softened steel called a die, using an instrument known as a burin or graver; it looks something like a bradawl. The engraver must be careful not to make any mistakes, or they will show up on the finished stamps; and if the burin does happen to slip, the mark it makes has to be erased and the line re-engraved.

When the die is fully engraved it is hardened and used to transfer the design to a small steel cylinder known as a roller. The transferring is done by rocking the softened roller, under great pressure, on to the flat die, so that the roller picks up the lines of the engraving, and is then known as a roller-die. You will see what a roller-die and its engraving look like by referring to the illustrations. After the transfer has taken place, the roller-die is hardened. It is then rocked, again with great pressure, on to a large, softened steel plate, the designs being impressed on the plate row by row as many times as there are to be stamps in the printed sheet. When this process (called 'entering' or 'laying down') is completed, the plate is hardened and may then be used for printing.

Egypt 5 paras with side panels transposed and inverted

Recess-printed stamp from U.S.A.

Mistakes can happen either during the laying down of designs on the plate or during printing. The designs are supposed to be perfectly straight, but sometimes one is laid down out of alignment. In that case it is erased, after which a fresh impression is laid down in place of the unsatisfactory design. This process is known as fresh entry. If any traces of the original impression remain on the plate, they will show up when the stamp is printed, and probably will result in part of the design being doubled. If, later on, you collect the early line-engraved issues of Great Britain, especially the Penny Black and imperforate Penny Red, you will come across many cases of such doubling.

Other varieties also occur on line-engraved stamps. In cases where a stamp is printed in two colours, and the centre and frame have to be printed in two operations, the centre might be printed upside down. This happens when the frame is printed first and the sheet is accidentally inverted before being put into the press a second time. An error like this can occur on stamps printed by methods other than line-engraving.

When a line-engraved plate becomes damaged or worn, it is necessary sometimes to repair it. Repairs may be made either by re-entering an impression immediately over the worn impression, so deepening and strengthening it, or else by drawing in or recutting by hand part of the worn or damaged impression. You may find stamps printed from the plate in its two different states: before and after repair. The recutting of frame-lines to strengthen them can be detected on a stamp, because the parts which have been recut will show up more prominently than the rest of the worn design.

**Recess printing**

Recess printing has been done sometimes directly from the engraved die or plate with-

Printed from a rubber
handstamp

## Surface printing

Printed from a copper
plate (Mauritius 1847)

Set up from printer's type

out transferring. The famous 'Post Office'
Mauritius were printed that way from a copper
plate.

When an engraved plate is inked, the colour
is forced into the lines of the engraving, and
during printing the paper and plate are
pressed together so that the paper picks up
the ink. You can recognize a stamp printed by
this method by passing your finger-nail
lightly across the surface, when you will feel
the ink standing up from the paper in little
ridges. If you look at the back of a modern
unused recess-printed stamp, you will see it is
pitted with hollows coinciding with the
raised lines on the front.

Recess printing, as you will have seen, is
printing from the recessed or sunken portions
of the plate. Typography is printing from
raised portions or the surface. There are
various kinds of surface printing, the simplest
being by making an impression with a rubber
stamp; this was done in 1886–7 for issues of
the New Republic of South Africa. Not much
more advanced is printing stamps on a typewriter, which was done in Uganda in 1895,
and in the occupied Turkish possession, Long
Island, in 1916.

Another simple form of surface printing is
to make impressions with a die cut in a hard
substance, such as metal, or even wood. An
engraving in wood was made in America
during the Civil War. At that time the Con-
federate States were cut off from the rest of
America and had to organize their own postal
services. Postmasters in a number of towns
made their own stamps, many of them being
in very simple designs, and printed by primitive methods. Grove Hill, Alabama, used an
engraving on wood, and the result can be
seen from the stamp illustrated.

An even more primitive design was used by
the postmaster of Hamilton, Bermuda, who

Made from a postmarking
handstamp with manuscript
addition (actual size)

Printed from stereotypes
(actual size)

Wood engraving
(actual size)

simply made some impressions of his post-mark on sheets of paper, wrote in the value, 'one penny', and signed each stamp. These postmasters' provisionals are extremely rare, and so are specimens of the first issue of Hawaii, the designs of which were set up from printer's type and ornaments.

Not all surface printing is as simple as this. A design can be engraved on a die, *en épargne* (that is to say, in relief), and although printing can be made directly from the die, this is not often done. Usually moulds are taken from the die, either in papier mâché or wax or lead.

When the papier mâché is used the method to be employed is known as stereotyping, and the design on the die is forced into wet papier mâché (or plaster) to form a 'mould'. When each mould has dried hard, molten metal is poured into it to form a 'stereo'. Stereos are then assembled to make a printing plate from which printings may be made. A well-known case of the use of stereotyping is the 1861 local provisional issue of the Cape of Good Hope, the so-called 'Woodblocks', which are not woodcuts at all. As a rule, stamps printed from stereotypes are not so highly finished as electrotyped stamps.

Wax (or lead) is used for the mould when electrotyping is to be used for making the printing plate. The die is impressed into the wax, and a thin coating of a conductor of electricity is put on the impression. The wax is then put in an electrotyping bath where a thin shell of metal is grown over the side bearing the impression. The shell is separated from the wax, strengthened and fitted to a wooden or metal base. Printing may then take place.

Collectors sometimes refer to a stereotyped or electrotyped copy of the die as a *cliché*.

These descriptions are of only the simplest forms of printing by these processes, and many

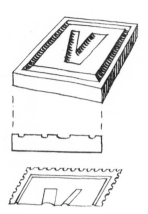

Recess

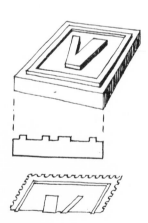

Surface

variations at all stages occur in practice.

Errors can occur during surface printing just as much as in any other process. Among such mistakes are errors of colour, where either a complete sheet is printed in the colour meant for another value, or where an electro or stereo of one value is accidentally assembled in the printing plate of another. An example occurred in each value of the 1d and 4d plates used for printing the Cape of Good Hope 'Woodblocks'. The 1d in blue and 4d in red are very valuable errors of colour.

Another variety found on surface-printed stamps is an inverted *cliché*, which results in what is known as a *tête bêche* pair, that is to say, a joined pair of stamps with one upright and its neighbour upside down. A variety of this kind is not always due to a mistake in assembling the plate. Some low values of Great Britain are printed purposely in panes with the right part upside down compared with the left so as to make it easier to bind the stamps into booklets. Of course, it was not intended to issue the stamps in *tête bêche* pieces, but in the case of the 2½d of 1958, some came into the hands of collectors. Other *tête bêche* varieties are found on the early issues of France and are rare ; but some European countries, such as Belgium and Germany, have issued *tête bêche* varieties in the usual way.

Tête-bêche pair

Surcharge

A double impression of the whole design or part of it can happen if a sheet is printed twice. An error like this usually turns out to be rare, and examples have occurred on stamps of Great Britain, such as the ½d of King Edward VII.

Overprints, which are words or a design applied to stamps after they are finished, but do not affect their value, and surcharges, which are words or figures printed on stamps after they are finished, altering or confirming the value, are very often surface printed, and although most overprints and surcharges are normal, sometimes inverted or double impressions occur, errors which most collectors delight in having.

Sometimes you can tell whether a stamp has been typographed by examining the back carefully. Especially in unused specimens you may find that the design, particularly the outer frame, is slightly indented into the paper and stands out at the back, not on the front like a recess-printed stamp.

### Lithography

Lithography is printing from a stone surface, and this method has often been used for producing stamps. The principle of lithography was discovered by a Bohemian, Alois Senefelder, in 1798. He found that if a polished limestone had a design drawn on it in printer's ink and the stone was wetted, it would attract the water in the uninked parts. Then, if an inked roller was run over the surface, the ink would stick to the design, but not to the watered parts of the stone. A sheet of paper could then be pressed on the stone and a copy of the design would come out on the paper.

Since Senefelder's time it has been found that metal can be treated and used instead of stone, and is much lighter and easier to handle. Some of the stamps described nowadays as being lithographed are really printed from metal plates bent around

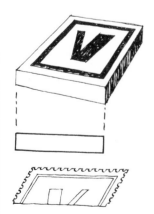

Lithography

The first lithographed
stamp, Zurich 1843

Photogravure

cylinders. The design is not usually drawn directly on the stone or metal. Sometimes the design is engraved on a metal die from which transfers are taken and built up on the stone either in blocks or singly ; sometimes transfers have been taken from the whole of a line-engraved plate containing many impressions.

Varieties occur in lithographed stamps, either before or during the transferring process, or else are caused by damage to the stone. Transfers are very fragile, and if one becomes creased or torn and is put on the stone without being noticed, the result will be what philatelists call a 'creased transfer'. In that case part of the stamp's design will be missing or defective. An example of a wrong transfer being put on a lithographic plate occurred in the 1940 issue of Thailand (Siam) where a 5 satangs error of colour is found in the sheet of 3 satangs stamps.

When metal is used instead of stone, a rubber 'blanket' is employed as a rule, between the metal and the paper. The 'blanket' is on a cylinder and as it revolves it picks up the impressions from the metal and transfers the designs to the paper. This method is known as offset-lithography, and was used, for example, to print the Egyptian airmail issue of 1933.

A lithographed stamp is completely flat, and shows neither indentations nor ridges on the front or back. The surface of an unused specimen may feel slightly greasy, and may appear shiny when held sideways to the light.

The photogravure printing process has been used for the low value stamps of Great Britain since 1934, and was first used for printing stamps in 1914. In one way this method is similar to recess printing, because the design is cut, or more correctly etched, into the plate or cylinder, but the ink does not stand up from the paper as in recess printing.

A modern lithographed stamp,
Netherlands Antilles 1966

Right, a letterpress stamp
with a photographic
half-tone in centre

Stamp printed by
photography

In photogravure the design is photographed repeatedly (as many times as there are to be stamps in the sheet) on to a photographic plate. The group of photographs is then reproduced in specially prepared gelatine on a sheet of paper, which is next squeezed on to a copper plate or cylinder and developed in warm water, leaving the gelatine designs on the copper. Etching fluid is then poured over the cylinder and eats away the unprotected copper. The cylinder is plated with chromium before printing takes place.

Photogravure stamps, especially unused copies, feel slightly velvety on the surface, due to the ink. The ink is very sensitive to petrol or benzine, and if a specimen printed by photogravure is put in petrol and the surface rubbed, the design will be smeared and sometimes almost obliterated.

Very occasionally stamps have been produced entirely by photography. The issues made in Mafeking during the siege of 1900 were done that way, and the reason why they are blue instead of black or brown and white is that a ferro-prussiate printing process was used. Sometimes a half-tone block has been used on a stamp. This is the kind of reproduction you will find in most newspaper or magazine illustrations, and if you examine them closely, you will see that they consist of tiny dots which go to make up the lights and shadows. In stamp production it has been mostly the centres which were printed from half-tone blocks, this being the case with the Bijawar set of 1937.

### Embossing

Embossing has been used since the early days of stamps, and the first issue produced by this method was the 2½ rappen of Basle, 1845. The dove in the centre was embossed in white on a blue background. In embossing, usually a die or matrix is engraved on steel, then hardened and used to make punches, which have the design in relief. These are known as male dies, and from them female dies are made, which have the design in recess, similar to the matrix. The two sets of dies fit into each other, and when a sheet of paper is put between them and pressure exerted the paper receives an embossed impression of the design.

Embossing can be either in plain relief, when no ink is used, or with parts of the design in colour, when the surface of the female die is inked.

An embossed stamp

Stamps issued during the British postal strike, 1971. Although not listed in general catalogues issues like these are of great postal-historical interest, and are among the first British decimal stamps

# 5 *Paper*

When you pick up a stamp and examine it,
you are almost sure to look at the design first,
then at the perforation, and last of all perhaps
at the paper on which the stamp is printed ;
but the paper might be the most interesting
part of the specimen.

Although many types of paper have been
used in stamp production, they are all
variations of only two main kinds, wove and
laid. If you hold a stamp on wove paper up to
the light, you will find that the texture is even,
and shows no particular pattern ; it is very
much like closely woven cloth. On the other
hand, a stamp on laid paper will show parallel
vertical or horizontal lines in it, rather similar
to a watermark.

This difference of texture occurs during
manufacture. All paper, whether machine-
made or hand-made, at some time is pulp, and it
is during the pulp stage that the texture is
determined. In machine-made paper the pulp
passes along the bed of the paper-making
machine and is squeezed by a wire roller known
as the 'dandy-roll'. If the wire is evenly woven,
the paper will be wove ; but if the roller
contains prominent vertical or horizontal wires,
the paper will be laid.

All the ordinary postage stamps of Great
Britain have been printed on wove paper,
although it has not always been of the same
kind. The embossed 10d and 1s issued in 1847
were on 'Dickinson' paper, which has silk
threads woven into the texture. This paper was
named after its inventor, John Dickinson, and
the object of the threads was to prevent the
removal of postmarks from used stamps ; any

Austria 1890 20 kreuzer
on granite paper
(enlarged x 2½)

*Paper*

attempt to erase the postmarks would loosen
the threads and tear the paper. Although this
invention worked well enough on imperforate
stamps, as soon as perforation was used the
threads became entangled in the pins of the
perforating machine. Switzerland, Bavaria and
Schleswig-Holstein have used silk-thread paper
as well as Great Britain.

In 1917 Britain printed her 8d stamp on
granite paper, which contains coloured fibres.
This paper is made by mixing bleached and
unbleached pulp, and the small fibres, looking
like coloured hairs, can be seen on the surface.
The high-value stamps of Jersey 1969 are
printed on granite paper, so were Austrian
high-value stamps of 1919–21 and many
issues of Switzerland among others. Granite
paper of poor quality was used in France
during the First World War, and is referred to as
*Grande Consommation.*

If you look at some of the imperforate 1d
red stamps issued by Great Britain from 1841
onwards, you will notice that they are on
blued paper. In order to obtain a good
impression of the design, the printers wetted
the paper before putting it in the press, and
impurities in the paper and printing ink
combined to make the bluish tone. In 1855
the 4d stamps appeared on blued paper, but
for not quite the same reason. At that time
De la Rue & Co., the printers, were experiment-
ing with solutions for coating the paper to
prevent the removal of postmarks. The coating
used on the 4d stamps contained.prussiate of
potash, which turned the paper blue.

The same firm printed the later issues
bearing the head of King Edward VII, and many
of them were on paper coated with a solution
containing a suspension of what collectors
and others thought was chalk but was barium
sulphide. This is known as chalky, or chalk-
surfaced paper, and you can usually recognize

it because it seems rather thick and has a glazed surface. Chalky paper was used for many British Colonial stamps printed by De la Rue & Co. During the First World War, when there was a shortage of coloured papers for some values, that firm put coloured surfaces on ordinary white paper: yellow for the 3d and 5s stamps, green for the 1s and 10s as well as chalk-surfacing. Stamps printed on this kind of paper are known as 'white backs', because the colouring is on the front only.

The coating of stamp paper as a safeguard against the removal of postmarks is not confined to Britain and the Colonies. Austria put a coating of diagonal bars of shiny varnish on her issues of 1899–1906, and Russia used crossed lines of surfacing in 1909. France and two of her colonies made use of *quadrillé* surfacing between 1892 and 1902.

If you look at the listing of New Zealand in Stanley Gibbons's big catalogue, you will find quite a large variety of papers mentioned there. For example, in 1862 pelure paper was used. This is very thin and semi-transparent, almost like rather thick tissue-paper but tougher, as pelure does not tear so easily, otherwise it would be useless for stamps.

In 1901–2 printings of the ½d and 1d values were made on Waterlow, Basted Mills and Cowan papers. These varieties are all wove, the first soft and the others rather thin and hard. Basted Mills paper takes its name from its manufacturers, the Basted Mills at Sevenoaks, Kent, and is so closely woven that it does not show the texture when held up to the light; Cowan paper reveals a texture of tiny diamond shapes.

During 1924–5 experiments were being carried out with other kinds of paper. They were Jones paper, which is chalk-surfaced and either thick or thin; De la Rue paper, of

Bars of shiny varnish on Austrian stamp (enlarged x 2½)

medium thickness and with or without chalk-surfacing; Cowan paper, different from that of 1901–2, thick and with a chalky surface; and Wiggins Teape paper, thin, hard and chalk-surfaced. You will get a better idea of the appearance of these different sorts of paper by examining specimens of the stamps themselves. Most of them are quite cheap, and their catalogue numbers range between S.G.519 and 535c.

Curious paper was employed in Latvia just after the First World War. There was a paper shortage, but large numbers of old German staff maps were found, and as the backs were blank, stamps were printed on them and were issued in 1918. If you have one of these 5 kopeck stamps, turn it over to see part of the map on its back. The next year Latvia issued stamps on exercise-book paper ruled with blue lines, and others on very thin, transparent paper, similar to cigarette paper. Later stamps were printed on the backs of unfinished bank-notes, so that the early Latvian issues provide plenty of variety.

The United States of America has used several different sorts of paper, such as the double paper tried experimentally in 1873. This consists of two thicknesses joined together, one thickness being very soft and porous, and it was on this, the upper layer, that the design was printed, the object being that any attempt to remove a postmark would destroy the paper's surface. Another type used in the USA was the blue rag paper on which stamps were printed in 1909. As its name suggests, this paper was made from rags and has a bluish tinge.

Very unusual paper was used for two stamps issued by Prussia in 1866. The paper is transparent and thin, and at one time collectors thought it was goldbeater's skin; that is why it is given that name in the

Latvian stamp printed on the back of a German staff map

Latvian stamp on back of banknote paper

catalogue. Really the paper is transparent because it was treated with resin. The stamp designs were printed in reverse on the back of the paper and show through to the front. The backs were gummed, and once the stamps have been stuck down it is impossible to remove them without damaging the design ; this, of course, was the object of using the resinized paper.

All the papers described so far have been wove. Some stamps exist on *bâtonné* paper, which, when held up to the light, shows parallel lines more widely set than those in ordinary laid paper. There are two varieties of *bâtonné* paper : wove *bâtonné*, where the spaces between the widely set parallel lines show a woven texture, and laid *bâtonné*, where these spaces show the texture of laid paper between the widely set *bâtonné* lines. Both kinds of *bâtonné* were used for stamps of the Indian Native State of Poonch in 1884. The famous Cape of Good Hope 'Woodblocks' of 1861 were printed on ordinary laid paper, so were Russian issues made between 1866 and 1905.

Fracturing gum to prevent paper curling (Photo by courtesy of the British Post Office)

# 6 *Watermarks and gum*

Many stamps are printed on watermarked paper, so that if you hold one of them up to the light, you will see a design or letters shining through in brighter patches than the rest of the paper.

'Watermark' is not really a correct term because it has little or nothing to do with water. In Chapter 5 you will have read how paper pulp comes into contact with the 'dandy-roll' as it passes along the machine. Sometimes, when paper is made, on the dandy-roll there are fixed small pieces of bent wire or metal shapes known as 'bits', and they impress themselves on the pulp and cause it to be very slightly thinner in those places. The 'bits' may be in the shape, for example, of crowns or letters, and in that case the paper will be watermarked in the same way.

In order to see a watermark, you will have to look at a stamp from the back and hold it up to the light. The watermarks on some stamps can be seen in that way, but others are more obstinate, so you will need a watermark detector. This is a black tray, or tile with a polished surface, which you can buy cheaply from almost any stamp dealer. If you place a stamp face downwards in the tray, you will usually be able to see the watermark clearly enough to identify it, but in particularly awkward cases you should pour a few drops of benzine into the tray with the stamp in it. Remember, though, that benzine is highly inflammable and extremely dangerous to use near a naked light such as a burning match, a cigarette or a fire ; even the vapour is liable to explode easily near a flame, so take precautions. The gum on the backs of unused stamps will not be affected by benzine, and as soon as it has evaporated they will be in the same state as before you poured on the liquid. Do not use benzine on stamps printed by photogravure or the designs may be spoiled.

There are four chief kinds of watermarks from the stamp collector's point of view : single, column (or simple), multiple (sometimes called alternate) and sheet. A single watermark is one in which only one 'bit' appears on each stamp. If you have any of the early line-engraved issues of Great Britain, the Penny Black, Penny Red or Twopence Blue, you will find that they have a watermark of this kind, and that it is either a small or a large crown.

Up to the reign of King George V all the postage stamps of Great Britain, except the small ½d of 1870, the 10d and 1s of 1847–54, had a single watermark ; the ½d was water-marked with the word 'halfpenny', which covers three stamps, and the 10d and 1s were unwatermarked. In 1912 the ½d and 1d of George V were issued on paper watermarked with the Royal Cipher GVR and a crown in column, that is to say, two watermarks appear, one above the other, on each stamp.

Later the same year those two values were printed on paper with a multiple Royal Cipher, in which the bits are arranged so that parts of several devices in alternate rows can be seen on every stamp. Since 1967 the stamps of Great Britain have been printed on unwatermarked paper. A multiple watermark is used in the Crown Colonies, and is known as Multiple Crown Script CA, to distinguish it from the Multiple Crown CA which was used before 1921. In the older watermark the crown is upright and the initials in block capitals ; in the modern version the Crown is rounded and the letters are in script. The initials CA stand for

Crown Agents. In 1956 a change in the watermark was made, and stamps issued from then onwards were watermarked with the St Edward's Crown above initials CA in large capital letters.

Sheet watermarks are rarely used nowadays but they are found on the older issues of some countries. A watermark of this kind usually appears in the centre of the sheet, and individual stamps show only a small part of the design or none at all. The 1854 issue of India had a sheet watermark of the arms of the East India Company and the words 'Stamp Office'; the Romanian arms covering 25 stamps appear in sheets of the 1900 issue of Romania.

Sheet watermark

Some watermark designs are curious and interesting. Multiple tortoises are found in the paper used for several issues of Tonga; Jamaica had a pineapple as its first watermark in 1860; and an elephant's head was used by India in 1865; Burma had multiple elephants' heads in 1938 and again in 1946. An umbrella is the strange watermark to be seen in many stamps of the Indian Native State of Cochin, while Travancore used a conch shell. A pyramid with the sun rising above it can be found on Egypt's first issue, and a honeycomb appears in the paper used for stamps of Danzig. The Cape of Good Hope long used

a cabled anchor as its watermark. These are only a few of the interesting devices which have been used as watermarks ; there are many others which you will enjoy finding yourself. For example, look at the stamps of South Africa, the Coronation long set of Newfoundland 1937, or the issues of Eire. All these have unusual watermarks, and will help to interest you in this fascinating side of stamp collecting.

Some watermarks are not quite what they seem. In order to be a true watermark, the device must have been worked into the paper in the way already described ; but Switzerland, for its issues between 1862 and 1898, used what is known as an impressed 'watermark'. This consists of a cross enclosed in an oval, which was embossed in the paper after it was made and is not really a watermark at all. Romania also used an impressed 'watermark' in 1889.

In 1924–5, when experiments with stamp paper were being carried out in New Zealand, some paper was too opaque to show a watermark clearly ; so the device NZ and a star, normally used now as the Dominion's watermark, was lithographed on the back of each stamp, usually in pale blue, but sometimes uncoloured or in black. Specimens of this pseudo-watermark are quite interesting, and you should make a point of obtaining one of the stamps for your collection.

Transvaal 1d 1905

Sometimes errors of watermark occur in stamps. One of the best known is found on the Transvaal 1d of 1905, which exists with the 'cabled anchor' of the Cape of Good Hope instead of the normal Multiple Crown CA. The stamps of Transvaal and the Cape of Good Hope were being printed by De la Rue & Co in 1905, and somehow a sheet of the wrong paper was used for a printing of Transvaal stamps. The error was not discovered until a philatelist in Transvaal noticed that a used 1d stamp bearing the Johannesburg postmark, was wrongly watermarked. His find started a treasure hunt, and a few other specimens of this error were traced, but no unused examples have ever been found because the post office where they came from had sold out before collectors knew about the variety. There is another and rarer error of watermark on the 10d stamp issued by Great Britain in 1867. At that time the watermark on British stamps was being changed from the heraldic emblems (roses, shamrock and thistle) to a spray of rose. The printers were instructed to print the 10d stamp (a new value) on the new paper, but instead they used the old paper for a small printing. Specimens of this error are very valuable and only about a dozen or perhaps less are known to exist.

**Gum**

If you look at the back of an unused stamp, you will nearly always find that it is coated with gum. Right from the beginning it was realized that the easiest way to fix a stamp to a letter was with gum, and what could be simpler than to put the gum on the stamp's back so that by moistening it the gum would become sticky?

Gum on the back of an unused specimen is important from a collector's point of view. Most collectors like to have stamps in perfect condition, and although this is not very hard to achieve with modern issues, it is much more difficult with older stamps which have passed through many collections. Each time an unused stamp is mounted it loses some of its original gum, and in time might lose all of it. Specimens like that are not very popular among collectors, and usually are worth less than stamps with full gum. That is why, whenever you put an unused specimen in your collection, you should take care to mount the stamp lightly. The reason why so much value is placed upon the gum is that it may be able to tell a story which the stamp itself might not do.

The gum used on many of the early stamps contained dextrine or potato starch, but nowadays pure gum is used much more often, and that on the backs of issues of Great Britain until 1968 was gum arabic; it is white and almost tasteless. Since then PVA (polyvinyl alcohol) gum has been used. It is not shiny and is almost invisible.

White gum has not always been used for stamps. In 1855 the backs of British embossed 6d stamps were coated with green gum. The gumming was done before the embossing, and some sheets had been embossed on the gummed side, so the use of coloured gum prevented mistakes of that kind, as it was easier to see which side of the paper had already been gummed.

The German state of Hanover used red gum on its stamps as early as 1850, and the issues of 1859 had rose gum. It is not known why coloured gum was used there, but perhaps the idea was that the stamp would leave a stain behind if it came unstuck from the letter and so would show that postage had been paid.

Nowadays, after paper has been gummed, the gum is usually broken up into tiny particles by a machine to prevent the paper from curling. The machine that does this is called a 'gum

Great Britain 1854 6d

German airmail stamp
of 1922–23

Economy gum on
German stamp

breaker' (see illustration on page 43). Sometimes a design is embossed on the gum for the same purpose. If you have any German stamps of the nineteen-twenties or -thirties, for example the airmail issue of 1922–3, look at their backs, and you will see that the gum has an embossed pattern of lines on it, and no less interesting is the gum on some local issues made in Germany after the Second World War; that has a honeycomb pattern, and is known as 'economy gum'.

Not all stamps are issued with gum on their backs. The Nicaraguan 1 centavo of 1937 was gumless, so was that country's Postal Anniversary set issued the same year. One printing of Gold Coast stamps made in 1884 was sent to the colony in ungummed sheets, because the humid atmosphere in West Africa had caused sheets of stamps to stick together. The first stamps of Uganda, which were produced on a typewriter, were issued without gum too. People wanting to stick them on a letter took them to a nearby gum-plant which provided the adhesive matter in a handy form.

Finnish stamp issued with
invisible gum

# 7 Methods of separation

If you look at almost any modern stamp, one of the first things you will notice is that the edges contain teeth. Not all stamps are like that, and if you had lived during the eighteen-forties, you might have seen quite a number of stamps, but all of them would have had plain edges, in other words, would have been imperforate, and if you had wanted to separate two or more of those stamps, you would have had to use scissors or a knife, unless you decided to tear the stamps apart.

Before stamps were provided with teeth, or perforations as collectors call them, that method of easily separating two pieces of paper was known, but it was due to Henry Archer, an Irishman, that perforation was applied to stamps. He invented a machine for that purpose about 1847, and wrote to the Postmaster-General stating what a boon it would be if all stamps were perforated. The Postmaster-General liked the suggestion, and

Imperforate

Imperforate miniature sheet

Archer carried out many experiments to improve the machine. Some of these tests were not only with perforation but also rouletting. In perforation, rows of small holes are punched in the margins between stamps, and the paper is cut right out of the holes ; but in rouletting, rows of short cuts are made and no paper is removed. You will read about rouletting later in this chapter.

Archer's experiments were successful, and in 1854 the world's first perforated stamps were issued officially by Great Britain. Since then almost every country has used perforation of some kind for its stamps.

In order to be able to punch holes in a sheet of stamps, a perforating machine contains a large number of flat ended pins. They are arranged in rows, and when the pins come down on the paper they cut right through it by pressure ; the cutting edges (the flat ends) of the pins enter holes that have been drilled to receive them. The pins and holes in different machines can be arranged in different ways, and the three different kinds of perforation known to collectors depend on the arrangement of the pins.

One kind is known as line perforation. In this the pins are fitted in long rows. The sheet of stamps is put into the machine and the pins cut through the spaces between the rows. All the horizontal rows might be punched first,

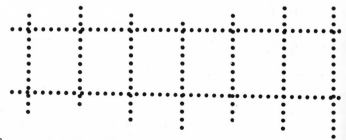

Line perforation

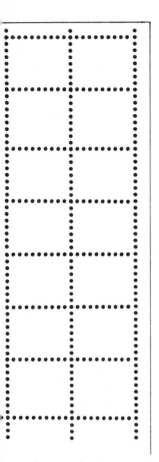

Comb perforation

then all the vertical rows, so that all the stamps will have perforations on the four sides. Where the horizontal and vertical rows cross each other the perforation will be a little irregular; that is how you can recognize a line-perforated stamp. Usually its corners will be uneven, some having rather too much paper attached to them, others being short and stumpy. Sometimes, particularly in the USA, line perforation is done by revolving wheels fitted with pins, and this process is known as rotary line perforation.

Another method is comb perforation. For this the pins are arranged in a long horizontal row with short vertical rows at right-angles to it, the distance between the vertical rows being the width of a stamp. The effect of one stroke of this machine looks like a comb with the teeth far apart. The machine begins perforating a sheet at the top row of stamps, and three sides of each stamp are perforated at one blow. The next stroke perforates the fourth side, and at the same time three sides of the next row.

The machine proceeds to cut row by row until the whole sheet is perforated. If there are twenty rows of stamps in a sheet the pins will have to descend twenty-one times, because the final stroke will cut the bottom of the last row and will go through the sheet margin as well. In comb perforation the corners of each stamp are usually even and regular. Frequently combs are used which perforate several rows at a time, and in these cases only the bottom of the rows of stamps is perforated on three sides, the stamps in the upper rows being perforated all round. Such perforation is known as 'multiple comb'

A third kind of perforation is known as harrow, and in this a whole sheet or a pane of stamps is perforated at one stroke. The corner of specimens perforated in this way are quite regular.

See if you can tell the difference between stamps perforated at least by line and comb machines, and then look for other variations. For example, perforation can be either clean cut or rough. Clean cut means that all the paper has been removed from the holes ; but in rough perforation part of the paper has been left behind and the holes are rather ragged. Some of the early British Colonial issues are often found with rough perforation.

If you have any of the surface-printed stamps of Great Britain issued about the eighteen-sixties or -seventies, you may find that some specimens look rather lopsided, because there is a wide blank margin at either the right or left. This blank space is known as a wing-margin. The sheets of stamps contained several small panes with broad margins between them, and the perforating pins were arranged so that they cut through part of each margin and left it attached to the adjoining stamps.

**Mistakes in perforation**

Mistakes sometimes occur in perforation, the commonest being misplaced perforation, in which the holes pass through part of the stamps where they were not intended. When this happens the specimens are off-centre or, in extreme cases, the perforations go through the centres of some stamps. Another error happens if the corner of a sheet becomes folded over before it is put through the perforating machine. In that case one or more stamps may have large, irregularly shaped pieces of paper attached to them (see illustration).

An interesting error which occurs rarely is 'imperf. between'. One or more rows in a sheet will be missed by the perforating pins, so that the stamps will have perforations on three sides but not on the fourth. Stamps like these are collected in pairs, with no perforations in the middle, and examples are usually valuable.

At times you will no doubt come across

Line perforation

Comb perforation

Clean-cut perforation

Rough perforation

Imperforate at top

Imperf. x perf.

South African pair perforated at the
edges and rouletted through the centre

British stamp with
wing margin

## Methods of separation

stamps with perforations only on two sides and imperforate on the other two. As a rule these specimens are from rolls of stamps, such as are used in stamp-vending machines.

If you have read any stamp journals or looked through a catalogue, you will have noticed that perforations are denoted by one, two, three or even four sets of figures with multiplication signs between, and perhaps you have wondered what they mean. Perforations are measured, not by the number of holes along each side of a stamp, but by the number in the space of 2 centimetres. Nearly always the top of the stamp is measured first, then the right-hand side, next the bottom, and finally the left.

This method of counting perforations was first described by Dr Jacques Amable Legrand, an early French collector, in 1866. He used a perforation gauge, similar to the type in use today, bearing several rows of black dots in parallel lines 2 centimetres long one above the other, and with each succeeding row containing one dot fewer than the row above. In order to gauge a stamp's perforation, you place the specimen on the gauge with one edge along a row of dots and move the stamp up or down the gauge until you find a row in which all the dots fit exactly into the perforation holes. The number at the side of that row is the gauge of the stamp's perforation, and would be expressed as, for example, perf. $12\frac{1}{2}$; that is to say, there are $12\frac{1}{2}$ holes in 2 centimetres.

If the gauge at the sides differs from that at the top and bottom, the perforation might be shown as perf. $12\frac{1}{2} \times 14$ and is called compound perforation. If a compound perforation is different on all four sides it will be recorded as $12\frac{1}{2} \times 14 \times 13 \times 15$ if those are its gauges.

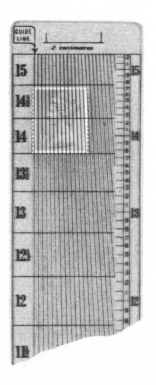

A modern gauge in which
the lines cut through the
point of each perforation

**Rouletting**     Rouletting, which has already been
mentioned, is not used very often nowadays,
but during the Second World War South
Africa, through economizing in paper and
issuing her small-size 'Bantam' stamps, was
obliged to use rouletting on them because the
usual perforating machines could not cope
with such miniature stamps. That is why you
will find these 'Bantams' perforated on two or
three sides and rouletted on the others.

There are more different kinds of rouletting
than there are of perforation. The simplest,
which was the kind used on the South African
stamps, is line rouletting, and is just a series of
short straight cuts, end to end. Line rouletting
is done usually after stamps have been printed,
and in this way is different from rouletting in
coloured lines, which takes place during the
printing. The cuts in that case are short and
straight, but have an outline of colour, the same
as that in which the stamp itself is printed.

Zig-zag rouletting is a series of short cuts
arranged obliquely in zig-zag formation, and
you will find examples in the 400,000 mark
provisionals issued by Germany in 1923.
Oblique rouletting is somewhat similar, except
that the cuts all run one way. Serpentine
rouletting, used for some early issues of
Finland, is a series of wavy cuts which, when
the stamps are torn apart, result in a serpentine
effect at the edges. Arc rouletting (or *percé
en arcs*) is a row of short semicircular cuts,
and when stamps rouletted in this way are
separated, the edges look as though they had
been perforated, but each tooth has a sharp
point instead of a rough or blunted end. Arc
rouletting was used on stamps issued by
Brunswick in 1865.

Pin rouletting (often wrongly called pin
perforation) is the type of cut which is made
when paper is put through a sewing-machine.
This type of roulette was used on some early

stamps of Barbados and Trinidad, and consists of small punctures very much like pin-pricks. Saw-tooth rouletting (or *percé en scie*) is a series of diagonal cuts slightly resembling a zig-zag roulette, but producing the effect of a saw's edge when the stamps are separated. Rouletting in crossed lines (or *percé en croix*) is a series of cuts in the form of the letter X, and when stamps rouletted in this way are torn apart they have irregular edges. The gauge of a roulette is measured in the same way as perforation, namely, the number of gaps or 'teeth' occurring in 2 centimetres.

Line rouletted stamp
from Schleswig-Holstein

Zig-zag roulette on a
German inflation provisional

Serpentine roulette

Rouletted Panamanian stamps on coloured paper
with special security lines in colour

# 8 Stamp designs

When you look at a stamp the first thing you see is its design. It may be the portrait of a king or queen, or perhaps a view of a city, a nation's flag, a bird, an animal or a coat of arms — possibly it is a scene from history. Whatever kind of design it is, no doubt you must have wondered why it came to be on the stamp, and who put it there.

A large amount of work is needed before a stamp design is chosen and ready for use. As a rule, when a new issue of stamps is contemplated, the Post Office sends invitations to several artists asking them to submit what they think would be suitable designs. The artists are given some guidance as to the kind of design required; for example, if the stamps are to celebrate a notable event, the artists will

Jersey commemorative issue designed by Jennifer Toombs, with one of her original sketches for the design

JERSEY 'Battle of Flowers'
5d
J. TOOMBS        COURVOISIER S.A.

be informed, and may also be told to include certain pictures, symbols or words in the design. In 1924, when artists were invited to submit a design for the Wembley Exhibition stamp of Great Britain, they were told that the words 'British Empire Exhibition 1924' must appear somewhere in the design.

Usually the artists make enlarged drawings of the designs, and supply smaller pictures to show how they will look in stamp size. The original drawings, which philatelists call artists' sketches, are very interesting, and if they can be obtained, make a fine addition to a collection. The drawings might not be used exactly as they are for the stamp designs, and it often happens that an artist is asked to make one or more alterations to his sketches before they are finally approved.

Stamp designs are not often the entirely original work of an artist. In many cases he will use as the chief part of the design a painting, photograph, statue or other subject. For example, in 1936 Bermuda issued a series of pictorial stamps, and the designs were all reproductions of photographs, most of them having appeared in an illustrated book about the Colony. The 2d value of this set caused some trouble, because it was supposed to show the *Viking*, a British-owned yacht which had won the Prince of Wales' Cup, but apparently the stamp engraver was given the wrong photograph to work from, and instead of the *Viking* the stamp depicts the American *Lucie*, whose performance was not as good.

This is not by any means the only mistake to have been made in a stamp design ; in fact, you would be able to form quite an interesting collection of stamps showing errors in the designs. When France issued her 90 centimes stamp in 1937 to honour the philosopher René Descartes, it was seen that in the design his famous work was described as '*Discours*

**Errors in design**

The *Lucie*

*sur la Méthode'*. Although that was correct in modern French, it was not the title which Descartes himself had given to the work, so a new stamp was engraved bearing the correct inscription, *'Discours de la Méthode'*, and was put on sale together with the earlier issue.

Error of inscription :
*'sur* la méthode' instead of
*'de* la méthode'

Another strange mistake concerns two stamps, one issued by the United States of America in 1893 and the other by Newfoundland four years later. The US stamp is the 3 cents of the Columbian series which shows a ship described on the stamp as the flagship of Columbus, the *Santa Maria*. The 10 cents of Newfoundland's Cabot series shows what is said to be Cabot's ship the *Matthew*; but examine the two stamps side by side, and you will get a surprise – both ships are the same. Something must have been wrong : perhaps the answer is that the ship on both stamps is neither the *Santa Maria* nor the *Matthew*, but simply a typical sailing-ship of the period.

There are mistakes on several other US stamps. One of them is in the inscription on the 1 dollar of the Omaha issue of 1898, where a herd of cattle is shown in a snow-storm, and at the foot of the stamp appear the words, 'Western Cattle in Storm'. This seems a suitable description, but it is not the real title, because the design was taken from a well-known painting by J. McWhirter, entitled, 'The Vanguard', and depicts a Scottish herd.

USA 3 cents
National Recovery Act

Two other strange mistakes can be seen on the 3 cents National Recovery Act stamp of 1933 and the 3 cents Transcontinental Railroad issue of 1944. The NRA stamp shows three men, representing a farmer, a miner and a business man, marching forward together, and the inscription at the foot reads, 'In a common determination'; but look at the business man, and you will see that he is out of step with the others! The railroad stamp shows a locomotive with smoke belching from its funnel. Compare the smoke with the flag waving at the right of the picture, and you will find that they are blowing in different directions, a freak of the wind which the artist probably did not intend.

The wind blows in two directions

There is another stamp which, for a long time, was thought to have a mistake in its design, but which is now known to be correct. The 5 cents issued by Newfoundland in 1866 depicts a seal on an ice-floe. It seems a rather ordinary seal until you look at its front legs; then you will see that it has feet! Whoever heard of a seal with feet instead of flippers? For many years collectors thought this a very funny mistake, but some years ago one philatelist discovered that the Great Grey Seal, a rare specimen which is found in

Seal with feet

Swedish 20 öre wrongly
inscribed 'Tretio' (30) on
lower stamp in pair, used
with a 30 öre on piece

Newfoundland, really does have forefeet – so
the designer was right after all.

So far only errors in the designing of stamps
have been mentioned, but there are others,
philatelic errors, which occurred during the
stamps' production, and it is that kind of
mistake which sometimes makes a rarity out
of a common stamp. A good example of a
philatelic error occurred on the Swedish 20 öre
of 1872–7. This stamp has the figures of
value in the centre and the words of value,
'Tjugo Öre', in a circular frame surrounding the
figures.

The stamps of this issue were printed from
*clichés* (you will have read about them in
Chapter 4), and one *cliché* in the plate of 20
öre became damaged, so it was cut out of the
plate and arrangements were made to
substitute another *cliché* for the damaged one.
The new *cliché* was to be soldered into the
plate, but before the work could be done, it
was found that no other *cliché* of the 20 öre
was available. So a 30 öre *cliché* was used,
the figures '30' were cut out and '20' were put
in their place : then the *cliché* was soldered
into the plate and printing was begun. Some
time after the stamps were issued it was seen
that, although '20' appeared in the centre,
'*tretio*' (thirty) was still in the circular frame.
This is a rare error, and collectors pay high
prices for examples of it.

Another type of error occurs when part of the design is omitted or printed incorrectly. In 1967 the 4d of Great Britain's Christmas issue was found with the gold printing left out, which meant that not only the value but also the Queen's head failed to print. This 'error' is one of many which occur from time to time in photogravure printing. A well-known instance of incorrect printing occurred on the USA 24 cents airmail stamp of 1918. That stamp was printed in two operations, the frame first, and the centre, showing an aeroplane in flight, next. One sheet was accidentally turned round before the centres were printed, so that all of them were upside down and showed the aeroplane flying on its back. Specimens of this inverted centre are highly prized, and they are worth several thousand pounds each.

Block of four from centre of sheet of USA 1918 24 cents air stamp with aeroplanes inverted

Railways

# 9 *Becoming a specialist*

Flowers

Space

When you have been collecting stamps for some time, perhaps three or four years, possibly longer, you will find that some parts of your collection have developed strongly while others are still weak ; that is to say, of several countries you may have fifty or a hundred stamps, and the pages of your album will be filled to overflowing, but other pages remain obstinately blank.

There may be several reasons for this unevenness. The stamps of some countries, especially the larger ones, are much easier to obtain than others, and obviously the issues of countries still using stamps will come your way much more often than obsolete issues. For example, you should be able to find 100 stamps from Great Britain or France before you can obtain one from, say, Saxony or Obock.

Another reason may be that the stamps of one or more countries appeal to you particularly, and you have tried harder to obtain new specimens from those countries. If that is so, you should begin to think about concentrating on them, in other words, collect and study their stamps only.

Specialization should be the aim of all stamp collectors. To some extent there is more fun in general collecting, because you may get a larger variety of stamp designs, colours and inscriptions ; but the real interest in philately lies in the specialized collection, where new discoveries are made, and where stamps which seem to be common varieties are shown by study to be rarities.

Music

## Becoming a specialist

If you feel attracted by the deeper side of stamps, as you probably will be after you have been collecting them for a few years, it is best to take stock of your collection with a view to choosing one or more countries on which to concentrate. There are advantages and drawbacks in the stamps of almost every country, and it may not be easy for you to make your choice right away, but perhaps the following notes will help you to decide. Some of the most likely countries are dealt with either individually or in groups, and although the final decision must rest with you, it may be as well to know in advance what difficulties you are likely to meet.

### Great Britain

1841 1d red

Queen Victoria 4½d
1892

If you live in the Mother Country, you are almost certain to have a large number of British stamps in your album; in fact, this may well be your 'strongest' country. Therefore, perhaps you will be toying with the idea of specializing in it. Great Britain is one of the most delightful, and at the same time one of the most difficult, countries in which to specialize. It is difficult, because it includes some of the world's greatest rarities, and there are sure to be many permanent blanks in your collection if you make this choice; another difficulty is that the condition of so many of the mid-Victorian stamps available to collectors is very poor, especially as regards the post-marks, which are nearly always heavy and smudgy. On the other hand, there is a huge range of types of stamps from which to choose, and from 1840 down to the present time no fewer than five different printing methods have been used to produce British issues, a range which is found in few other countries.

The classic Penny Black and Penny Reds provide a field of study in themselves, and, at least as far as the Penny Reds are concerned, although a great deal has already been written

King Edward VII issue

King George V

King George VI

about them, much original work remains to be done. There is still plenty of material about fairly cheaply, and if you want to take up the study of the imperforate Penny Red, you will find many fellow enthusiasts in all parts of the country engaged on the same task.

An issue which has generally been neglected but is rapidly coming into its own and offers scope for study is the 1887–92 series, where many plate varieties, shades and other differences still wait to be discovered. The Edward VII issues, too, are full of interest, so are the George V types of 1911–12, 1912–22 and 1924–6, nor is the photogravure issue of 1934–6 unworthy of attention. There is considerable interest in the stamps of George VI, and quite a substantial collection can be built up of all their varieties of printing and watermark. The issues of Elizabeth II are very popular and a specialized collection of them can be fascinating.

The study of British postmarks is an immense field, and there is also considerable uncharted territory among the so-called 'Cinderellas', such as telegraph stamps, locals and postal stationery. Great Britain offers variety and varieties almost unlimited, but if you take it up you must be prepared never to be able to attain completeness.

Queen Elizabeth II

Commemorative multicoloured
postmark for Philympia 1970
(actual size)

**Australia**

Australia is a wonderful country for collectors. The recent issues are pictorial and show flowers, animals, people and scenes from Australian history. The stamps are colourful and finely printed. Many of the earlier issues, although less picturesque, contain numerous varieties well worth studying. Apart from the high values and a few rarities, most of the stamps are cheap, and can be bought in large quantities without much difficulty, so that there is plenty of material for study.

**India**

Among collectors outside India and Pakistan, this is one of the less popular eastern groups. The early lithographed issues of 1854 have been fairly well studied and books written about them, but the earlier twentieth-century stamps have been comparatively neglected,

India 1947

Indian stamp used at Aden

and this may be because of their not very interesting designs. However this has been more than balanced by issues made since independence was granted in 1947. Material is plentiful and cheap, and if you feel the romance of the East, you might do far worse than specialize in Indian stamps. There is great scope, too, in the field of Indian postmarks, and although a few books have been written on this subject, there is much still to be learned.

**West Indies**

This is one of the most popular groups in the Commonwealth, and much variety is offered to the collector who chooses these stamps for his speciality. One of the disadvantages is that some of the early issues are rare and valuable, so that you must be prepared for blank spaces in your collection. The early stamps of countries such as Barbados, St Vincent, St Lucia and Trinidad were printed by Perkins, Bacon & Co, and if you are keen on these miniature works of art, you will gain much enjoyment from collecting them, provided that you can afford them. If you prefer gaily-coloured pictorials, you will find enough to interest you in the modern series, which in many cases have the advantage of being fairly cheap, except for some of the

St. Vincent 1880, a classic design by Perkins, Bacon & Co.

Trinidad and Tobago

Barbados

commemorative issues. Another point to bear in mind is that the stamps in this group, being so popular, are a good investment, and if you keep an eye on the value of your collection, you can take up these issues safely in the knowledge that provided you buy only fine specimens, your collection will grow rather than diminish in value.

**South Africa**

Natal

Orange Free State

South Africa

Before the Union of South Africa was formed in 1910, the four provinces issued their own stamps. There were separate issues for the Cape of Good Hope, Orange Free State, Natal and Transvaal. Those stamps offer a large collecting scope, even though a lot of work on them was done years ago. As the provinces no longer have stamps of their own, they are philatelically 'dead' countries, and with one exception are not very popular with collectors. Nothing sustains interest in a country's stamps so much as periodical new issues. Despite their unpopularity, the issues would make a good field for specialization if you are keen on studying stamps from the philatelic angle. Between 1869 and 1895 Natal issued many varieties of overprints which make a study in themselves, and the same applies to the Orange Free State and Transvaal, even though books have been written about both these provinces in fairly recent years. The Cape of Good Hope also has much to offer the specialist, not only in its romantic triangulars, which may be beyond your purse, but in the later typographed stamps. Only the fringe has been touched by present-day collectors in Africa and Great Britain in studying the modern issues of South Africa, with their different printing methods, and as material is cheap, you can take up that country without too much strain on your finances.

**Europe**

France
'Peace & Commerce'

Austria

Cyprus

There are many specialists in most of the countries of Europe, and it is true that a country's stamps are more popular in that country itself than anywhere else. French stamps are among the favourites, not only in France, but outside it. The early issues of France, like those of many other countries, include some great rarities, but there are plenty of cheap and interesting stamps in the series after the first. If you like stamps in which plate flaws abound, you should take up the 20 centimes of 1853 or 1862. The 'Peace and Commerce' type of 1876–1900 lends itself to study, so, perhaps, would the picturesque modern commemoratives; early French postmarks too are a fascinating study.

Belgium presents most interest in its early issues, but there are possibilities about the 1915–22 series. Holland's greatest attractions lie probably in the issues between 1867 and 1891. Germany is a vast and complicated field, with its many stamp issuing states, and this certainly provides ample scope for specialization; the same applies to Italy and the Italian states. Austria has possibilities, especially as some values in the early sets are obtainable at low prices, and there is a fine range of postmarks which, although they have been studied, offer pleasure and satisfaction to the philatelist with the knowledge needed to pick out scarce varieties from among common material. One of the drawbacks of collecting early European stamps is that there are many forgeries about, and until you have gained sufficient experience, you had better be careful if you do not want to be sorry. However, you will be safe if you obtain your specimens only from reliable dealers, who will guarantee everything they sell.

Arrival of Lafayette

Pony Express commemorative

Stephen Collins Foster,
composer of
*The Old Folks at Home*

## USA

The stamps of the United States of America are popular all over the world but, like other countries, they enjoy the greatest popularity in the USA itself. In fact comparatively few collectors there are concerned with any other issues. The stamps themselves present many features of interest. The early Postmasters' provisionals are nearly all extremely rare, and although that description cannot really be applied to the first governmental issue of 1847, those two stamps, 5 and 10 cents, are not likely to appeal to collectors with a limited amount of money to spend. There are plenty of interesting stamps among the middle issues (1870–88) and the different printings present a fascinating field of study. The early commemorative series are becoming more and more expensive, especially in fine condition, but the modern commemoratives, with their designs illustrating so many phases of American history, are still very cheap and plentiful, and a picturesque collection of them can be formed without much difficulty.

Once you have decided upon a country or group in which to specialize, and there are many others quite as interesting as the few mentioned here, try to read as much about it as you can. Articles and books have been written about the stamps of most countries, and if you do not read them, you may be going over ground already covered by other philatelists instead of continuing where they ended. You will see in Chapter 12 hints on how to find out what has been published.

left to right: New Zealand, Chile
Portugal
Rwanda Republic, Austrian Levant
used at Jaffa
Congo Republic, Norway, and Japan

'Head leaning too far forward', comment on an essay of King Edward VII, whose initials appear at the top of the sheet

## 10  *Not only stamps*

The most important part of a stamp collection is the stamps; but there are many other interesting items which belong to a specialized collection and which cannot really be called stamps. They include essays, proofs, colour trials, imprimaturs, specimen stamps, artists' sketches and so on. None of these should be put in a general collection, but they can add great interest to one that is specialized.

In the first place you will no doubt want to know what all these different terms mean, and how you could recognize one of the examples

**Essays**  if you were to see it. An essay is a suggested design for a stamp not issued. When it is intended to make a new issue of stamps,

Essay for
Great Britain
stamp 1879
(actual size)

artists are usually invited to submit what they think would be suitable designs. The designs might be either in stamp size or larger, and sometimes printed, but more usually are drawn by hand. All the designs submitted are considered by a committee which selects one or more, and they are eventually sent to the printers, who use them, perhaps slightly altered, as the stamps' designs.

It is very interesting to be able to show the progress of a design by including artists' sketches and essays in your album, but the drawback is that most items of that kind are extremely rare, and unless you can afford to pay quite high prices for them, you may have to do without. However some essays, of which fairly large numbers were made, are not too expensive, and you may be lucky enough to find a few for your collection. That depends to a large extent on what country or group of stamps you collect. Few essays of British stamps are cheap, but those of some less popular foreign countries can be obtained without very much difficulty.

## Stamps not issued

Prepared for use
but not issued
(a colour trial in
grey for the
2d 'Tyrian Plum')
– actual size

Rather similar to an essay is a stamp which was prepared for use but not issued. In 1910 the British Post Office was about to issue a new 2d stamp when King Edward VII died. The stamp was never put on sale at post offices, but a very small number of specimens have come into the hands of collectors. This stamp was printed in a deep purple colour, and is known to philatelists as the 'Twopence Tyrian Plum'. Another stamp prepared for use but not issued was the British 1½d printed in rosy mauve. This stamp was to have appeared in 1860, and supplies were ready, but the issue was deferred for ten years. The old stock was not used then, but the stamp was printed in another colour, rose-red. Examples in rosy mauve are rare, because nearly all specimens in that colour were destroyed.

*Not only stamps*

### Die proofs

Great Britain 1860 the unissued 1½d rosy-mauve. The stamp was issued in rose-red in 1870.

After the approval of a design, the printers set about making a die, as you will have read in Chapter 4. During this process a number of proof impressions may be taken, and if you are able to obtain any proofs of that kind, they will add to the interest of your collection. Items like that are, of course, usually obtainable from stamp dealers.

If a proof is taken from a die, it is known as a die proof, or sometimes as an engraver's proof; but if taken from the finished plate, it is a plate proof, or perhaps a colour proof. You will be able to recognize a die proof because it will be just one stamp, usually printed in black on card, and with large margins all round, in fact so large that the stamp could not possibly have been used on a letter in that state. Therefore you will see that a die proof is one impression in the centre of a card. Sometimes the card will have a few words on it, such as, in the case of certain British and Colonial die proofs, 'Before striking' or 'After hardening', these words referring to the condition of the die at the time

Die proof for Guatemala

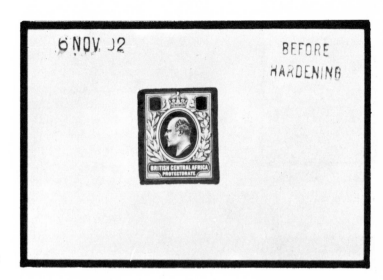

Die proof of
British Central Africa

when the proof was taken. In other cases
there may be just a date or initials.

Proofs are not always of the whole design.
Often they show only a centre or a frame, or
perhaps the portrait to appear on a stamp.
At other times a proof might be taken of the
whole stamp without the inscriptions, or of
the inscriptions alone without the stamp.
If you are fortunate enough to obtain several
proofs, each showing a different part of the
stamp, you will want to put them all in your
album, with appropriate writing up, to show
the progress of the work.

**Plate proofs** When the plate has been made, proofs are
taken from that too. As a rule they are in black,
and are nearly always imperforate; but sometimes proofs are made in various colours so that
the shade most suitable for the stamps can be
**Colour trials** chosen; these coloured proofs are referred to
as colour trials. Usually plate proofs and colour
trials are less rare than die proofs, because
whole sheets of plate proofs are printed,
whereas die proofs are made one at a time,
but that does not mean to say that proofs of
any kind are as easy to find as ordinary stamps.

Great Britain Specimen

Plate proofs and colour trials are often on white, but sometimes on tinted paper. For example, a colour trial of the King Edward VII 2½d stamp of Great Britain was printed in purple on blue paper, similar to the Queen Victoria 2½d of 1887–92, but the issued stamp was in blue on white paper. Then some plate proofs of the Edwardian series exist in the issued colours on buff paper, and of the Queen Victoria 1887–92 ½d and 3d on green paper. As you gain philatelic knowledge and experience, you will be able to recognize proofs when you see them, and may be able to secure some for your collection.

Italian proof
overprinted Saggio

Puerto Rico with
Muestra overprint

**Specimen stamps**

Transvaal
overprinted Monster

Before stamps are actually put on sale, examples are sent to the Universal Postal Union at Berne for distribution to other countries. This is done so that when letters bearing the new stamps reach foreign parts, there is no query about the stamps being a fraudulent issue. Before they were sent to Berne the specimen stamps were usually overprinted or perforated with the word 'Specimen' or its equivalent in other languages. For example, in Spanish the word is 'Muestra', in Italian 'Saggio' and so on.

Specimen stamps are often impressions from the plate in an early state, and are in shades used at the beginning of each particular

Proof from a small plate of 12 stamps for
experimental purposes with experimental cancellation

issue's life. Therefore, such specimens are
useful for comparison in cases where shades
vary in later printings of the same stamps.
As a rule it is not very difficult to obtain
examples of specimen stamps, because there
is a limited demand for those which come on
the market, and usually only stamps which are
rare in normal state fetch substantial prices
when overprinted 'Specimen'.

# *Some philatelic terms*

A pair se-tenant

A provisional

A souvenir or miniature sheet
(actual size)

Stamp with part
marginal inscription
(actual size)

A bisect: the Great Britain 1840 2d blue cut in half
and used for 1d (actual size)

Portrait and value
omitted
(actual size)

Value omitted
(actual size)

Used on piece and tied
by postmark (actual size)

## 11  *Writing up*

When you begin to form a specialized collection, you will find that an ordinary printed album is of no use to you. In the first place, there will be pages for the stamps of many countries which you no longer collect, and secondly, there will not be enough room for the issues of your favourite country. What you will need is an album with loose leaves and blank pages, blank, that is to say, except for a faint *quadrillé* pattern.

Of course, you will not want to keep the pages blank. Besides the stamps you mount on them, you should provide the pages with details such as the date of issue, perforation, watermark and other particulars about the stamps; in other words, you will have to write up your collection. Writing up presents a bigger problem to some collectors than others; but if your handwriting is neat or you can form printed characters easily, you will enjoy doing this work on your album.

To be effective, writing up must be not only neat but interesting. It must tell the story of the stamps on the page, no more and no less, although you will have to use your own discretion where to begin and end. If you over-elaborate, and fill more of the page with writing than stamps, it will distract attention from your specimens instead of drawing it to them. On the other hand, it is advisable to put more than simply the date of issue at the top of each page.

No hard-and-fast rules can be set down about the exact details to put in the writing up. Most collectors begin with the date of issue, following that with the watermark, perforation, printing method, name of the printer and designer. You will find most or all of these particulars in the catalogue, but in some cases you may have to search farther afield, in handbooks.

Aa Bb Cc Dd Ee Ff Gg

Hh Ii Jj Kk Ll Mm Nn

Oo Pp Qq Rr Ss Tt Uu

Vv Ww Xx Yy Zz & £

1 2 3 4 5 6 7 8 9 10 .,

*Aa Bb Cc Dd Ee Ff Gg Hh Ii Jj Kk*

*Ll Mm Nn Oo Pp Qq Rr Ss Tt Uu*

*Vv Ww Xx Yy Zz 1234567890.*

Before you do any writing at all on the album page, arrange the stamps you wish to put on that page but do not mount them. When they are arranged to your satisfaction, plan the writing up to go with them; if necessary, write it roughly on a piece of scrap paper and imagine how it will look on the album page. Then, when you are nearly ready, take all the stamps away and put them in a safe place before you begin the writing. Some philatelists could tell a sad story of stamps ruined through spilt ink.

Before you begin writing, test the nib with a few preliminary letters on a spare sheet of paper. That will help you to get used to the pen and may avoid mistakes as soon as you put it on the album page.

Although your handwriting may be extremely neat, you might want to try a fancy script, and if you are uncertain of the way to form any letters, you should read *How to arrange and write-up a stamp collection*, by Stanley Phillips and C. P. Rang published by Stanley Gibbons Ltd, where, in Chapter 7, you will find many useful hints on lettering.

If you cannot undertake to write up your collection neatly enough, there are three possibilities open to you. The first is to get someone else to do it for you. If you have a friend or relation who is expert at neat writing, perhaps you will be able to persuade him or her to undertake the work; if not, you could go to a firm of dealers who specialize in writing up collections, but this will be expensive, and unless you are prepared to spend pounds, you had better adopt another method.

The second possibility is to use writing-up labels, which can be obtained from almost any stamp dealer. They are gummed slips of paper bearing printed words of the kind used when writing up a collection. All you have to do is to cut out the words and to paste them on the album page as desired.

There is, of course, a limit to the amount of 'writing up' you can do in this way, that limit being set by the words printed on the labels. For example, whereas if you were actually writing you might put 'Proofs of these stamps exist in red, black, green and blue', you might have to be satisfied with only the word 'Proofs' if you use labels. Another disadvantage of gummed labels is that they do not look nearly as neat when stuck on to a page as

1858–79

Watermark Large
Crown

Perforation 14

Letter in each
corner

Plate No. 71    Plate No. 72    Plate No. 73

does a well-formed handwritten lettering, but
there is no doubt that labels are better than no
writing at all.

The third possibility is to do the 'writing up'
on a typewriter. If you have access to a
machine and can type reasonably well, you
will be able to obtain pleasing results with a
little trouble. When 'typing up', it is best to
write all the particulars on a sheet of paper and
then work out the exact number of characters
(letters and spaces) to be put in each line.

When typing on the album page, leave a
reasonably wide margin at the left and allow
for an equivalent space at the right. If your
typewriter is equipped with a wide carriage,
you should be able to insert the album page
without folding ; but if the carriage is of the
usual width, you will have to fold over the
left-hand margin of the page in order to get
it into the typewriter. Do this folding with
care, and see that the paper does not become
crumpled as you put it in the typewriter ; then,
when you take the page out again, you will be
able to unfold it easily and put it back in your
album.

## 12  *Reading about stamps*

Magazines

More has been written about stamps and stamp collecting than probably any other hobby, but the average collector does not take advantage of the vast store of knowledge at his disposal. It is a fact that most collectors would rather spend £1 on a stamp than a tenth of that amount on a book to increase their knowledge and enjoyment of stamps, and many people miss the real pleasure and interest of philately by not reading even a few stamp periodicals regularly.

There are more than a dozen stamp magazines published regularly in Great Britain, and they contain articles catering for collectors of every kind, from the beginner to the advanced specialist. Many of these magazines can be bought from newsagents or bookstalls, but some are obtainable only by subscription from the publishers.

Among the periodicals you are almost sure to have seen at one time or another are *Stamp Monthly*, *Philatelic Magazine*, *Stamp Collecting*, *The Stamp Lover* and *The Stamp Magazine*.

*Stamp Monthly* is issued by Stanley Gibbons Ltd, and enjoys a wide sale among philatelists of all classes. It contains popular and specialized articles, notes on forthcoming issues of stamps, and a new issue chronicle in the form of supplements to Gibbons's catalogues.

*Philatelic Magazine* is a monthly, and its contents include new issue notes, some articles of a specialized nature and others of general interest, book reviews and similar material likely to appeal to collectors.

*Stamp Collecting* is a popular newspaper which includes early news and pictures of new stamp issues, as well as notes about important events in the philatelic world, brief reports of societies' meetings and articles on general philatelic topics.

*The Stamp Lover* is the journal of the National Philatelic Society, containing popular and research articles and notes, as well as an 'Index to Current Philatelic Literature', which lists the contents of more than 100 different magazines printed in English throughout the world.

*The Stamp Magazine*, a monthly, contains a detailed guide to new issues, several articles, some more advanced and others for beginners, a financial page, and occasionally reprints of important articles appearing in overseas magazines.

Among the magazines with which you may not be so familiar can be mentioned : *The London Philatelist*, organ of the Royal Philatelic Society, London, containing important research articles ; *Philatelic Journal of Great Britain* ; *The Philatelist* ; and a number of others each with its own particular features.

To book a subscription to every magazine, or even to buy each one regularly from a newsagent, will probably cost more than you can afford ; but you should certainly try to obtain two or three regularly, and no doubt you can refer to others in your local public library or stamp club. Most stamp clubs have libraries of their own, and subscribe to several magazines which members can read in the club-room, so that it will be worth your while joining a club. Stamp clubs are discussed in the next chapter.

If you specialize in any country, you will certainly need to subscribe to several magazines and read them regularly. Should you fail to do so you may miss reading about important new

**Books**

discoveries and researches in the stamps in which you specialize.

Besides reading the periodicals, though, you should read also the handbooks, because they contain the fundamental knowledge about the countries with which they deal. The literature of philately is so vast that there would not be enough room in this book to give even a quarter of all the publications that have appeared since the eighteen-sixties. In 1911 a

**Catalogues**

catalogue of the Earl of Crawford's library appeared, containing details of almost every philatelic book, magazine and catalogue ever published. That catalogue was practically complete up to 1908, and consisted of more than 920 columns of listings, with large foolscap-size pages. Since then, at least thrice as much philatelic literature again has been published, so that you can imagine how huge a complete catalogue of it would be.

A very large amount has been written about the stamps of philatelically popular countries, such as Great Britain, the USA, France and Germany, but less about the comparatively small countries like Monaco, Luxembourg, Bulgaria and so on. It may be that no hand-books have been written about your favourite stamps; if that is the case, you will have to be content with articles, and perhaps, in due course and after years of study, you may be able to write a handbook yourself.

In order to find out what handbooks and articles have been written about your country, you will want to refer to an index. A number of indexes to philatelic literature have been compiled at various times, some being general and others specialized. One of the best is the *Standard Index to Philatelic Literature*, published by Harris Publications Ltd, in 1926. This index is arranged in alphabetical order of countries, with subheadings of stamp issues according to dates, followed by special subjects. The chief articles in more than 40 important magazines, as well as most of the leading handbooks in a number of languages, are listed in this index. Although it has not been brought up to date and its usefulness tends to grow less with the passing of time, the *Standard Index* is an outstanding and valuable key to the literature of stamp collecting, and you should not fail to consult this work at your public library whenever you need information on a philatelic subject.

Less ambitious is the *Philatelic Index*, published in 1925 by the Philatelic Congress of Great Britain, for it covers only about 20 magazines, and with a few handbooks in an Appendix. Indexes have been published also to the first 77 volumes of the *London Philatelist*, the first 75 volumes of the *Philatelic Journal of Great Britain*, the first 50 volumes of *The Stamp Lover* and the first 20 volumes of *The Philatelist*. All these are necessary works, and if you cannot obtain them from your local library, you should be able to refer to them in the library of your stamp club.

**Libraries**     Most stamp clubs have philatelic libraries, some of them being very fine collections indeed. Probably the world's largest accumulation of philatelic literature is that of the Collectors' Club, in New York, consisting of about two million items. This figure includes individual numbers of magazines, so that in the case of a monthly journal one year's issues, comprising one volume, count as twelve items.

A splendid library belongs to the Royal Philatelic Society, London, and is housed at the Society's premises at 41 Devonshire Place. The library contains some of the greatest rarities of philatelic literature, early books, magazines and catalogues, which were not thought much of in the days when they appeared, and later became almost unobtain-

.able. Besides the rarities, most of the world's philatelic magazines and handbooks are almost complete in this library.

The National Philatelic Society has a fairly large library, not as extensive as that of the Royal Philatelic Society, London, but containing most of the works an average philatelist is likely to need. The library at the British Museum is world-famous, but perhaps you do not know that it includes a large and valuable section containing philatelic literature. That library contains the fine collection formed by the Earl of Crawford, which was bequeathed to the Museum on the Earl's death in 1913.

There are also a number of private collections of philatelic literature in existence, among which can be mentioned those formed by George T. Turner, the late Fred. J. Melville, founder of the Junior Philatelic Society, and the late Dr Emilio Diena ; the Melville library was bought by the Library of Congress in the USA. The authors have a library of approximately the same size as that of the National Philatelic Society.

Although the chief use of philatelic literature is to publish information for the benefit of collectors in general, there is almost as much fascination in collecting rare stamp books as there is in collecting stamps. It is most interesting to browse among old stamp journals and catalogues published in the eighteen-sixties and to compare conditions in the stamp world then and now.

The forerunner of the catalogue was a lithographed list of stamps, produced in 1861 by Oscar Berger-Levrault of Strasburg, and later that year Alfred Potiquet, a French civil servant, compiled what was to be the first printed stamp catalogue ever published. In Great Britain Frederick Booty, of Brighton, brought out a catalogue entitled, *Aids to Stamp Collectors*, in 1862, and in the same year appeared *The Monthly Advertiser* (later *The Stamp Collectors' Review and Monthly Advertiser*), the world's first philatelic magazine, product of a Liverpool firm of stamp dealers. All these early publications are now extremely rare, and the few copies available are keenly sought by collectors of philatelic literature.

# 13 *Joining a stamp club*

Although the actual collection and study of stamps is the most important part of philately, there is another branch of activity in which many collectors take part: the social side. Stamp collecting lends itself to almost endless discussion, so that it is not surprising to find large numbers of stamp clubs in all civilized countries. These clubs range from small local gatherings, with a dozen or so members, to national societies, whose membership runs into thousands and extends all over the world.

The largest organization is the American Philatelic Society with a five-figure membership. This Society is rather different from most others, for it does not hold regular meetings, but conventions are organized in different parts of America at which several hundred members gather. The Society publishes a monthly magazine, *The American Philatelist,* and also runs an exchange section.

The oldest and most famous society is the Royal Philatelic Society, London. Founded in 1869 by some of the pioneers of stamp collecting in England, this Society is looked upon by the philatelists of all countries as the world's premier society of its kind. Its membership includes most of the leading philatelists. For many years King George V, himself an enthusiastic philatelist, took an active interest in the Society's affairs. After he ascended the throne, it became a custom for the Society's first meeting in each season to be honoured with a display of stamps from the Royal Collection, with a commentary by the curator, and this practice has been continued ever since.

The home of the Royal Philatelic Society,

London, is at 41 Devonshire Place, W.1, and there the monthly meetings are held. The library is open to all members, so is the 'museum', an interesting collection of philatelic relics which include the original plates used for printing the 'Post Paid' stamps of Mauritius. The Society has an Expert Committee, which for a fee pronounces on the genuineness or otherwise of stamps submitted for examination. All specimens considered genuine are photographed and granted a certificate with the photograph attached.

The National Philatelic Society, with headquarters at 44 Fleet Street, London E.C.4, is the largest organization of its kind in the Commonwealth, having a membership of several thousands.

Meetings are held regularly in London during the season, and it is by no means unusual for 100 or 150 members to be present. There is a bourse and auction at most meetings, followed by a display of stamps. The displays are usually selected pages from important collections, but all members of the Society are invited to display interesting items from their collections, and there is an annual competition for the NPS Cup, which is awarded for the best exhibit on Members' Day.

The Society runs an exchange branch, through which members circulate books of stamps they have for sale and receive parcels of stamp books from which they can buy. The library has already been mentioned ; another advantage of membership (which costs £5 a year) is that any member can submit six stamps for examination by the Expert Committee free of charge. The Society's journal, *The Stamp Lover*, is sent free to members.

There are so many local stamp clubs that it is impossible to mention them all here, but you will find a list of active societies in the *Philatelic Societies' Year Book*. Nearly all these clubs welcome new members, and it will help you to get more pleasure out of stamp collecting if you communicate with the secretary of your nearest club and become a member of it.

Many of the local clubs are affiliated to the Philatelic Congress of Great Britain, which in itself is not a society, but holds a yearly convention attended by delegates of the member clubs and by philatelists who belong to the Congress. At this convention, papers are read, stamp topics discussed, the Roll of Distinguished Philatelists is signed and other social functions held.

Many clubs organize local exhibitions of stamps, and every ten years or so an international exhibition is held in London, besides two annual national stamp exhibitions. Although you may not be able to display any stamps, you should make a point of attending every stamp exhibition you can. At exhibitions stamps will be on view which otherwise you might never be able to see, and the more stamps you can inspect the greater will your philatelic knowledge become.

It is from the international exhibitions that you are likely to reap the most benefit. These shows attract entries from all over the world, and the cream of the finest collections is displayed for competition, prizes being awarded for the best entries in each class. By inspecting the exhibits you will see how specialists arrange their stamps, noting the important points about each specimen by writing up, sketches, photographs and so on. You will see also some of the rarest stamps; if you are lucky the most valuable of all, the British Guiana 1 cent of 1856, as well as one or more of the 'Post Office' Mauritius and similar rarities. Do not expect to see the whole exhibition at one visit. Try to go there at least two or three times.

Another reason why you should visit exhibitions is that you will meet other collectors and dealers. At most exhibitions there are dealers' stands where stamps can be bought. By making a few purchases you will be able to get into conversation with the dealers, who will be only too pleased to help you with your collection, provided that you do not take up too much of their time while they are busy. If you are keenly interested in stamps, you should not find it very difficult to get introductions to other philatelists. Perhaps one of the dealers will be able to introduce you to collectors who are visiting the exhibition at the same time as you are, and by making these contacts you will increase your philatelic knowledge.

Many museums have stamp collections. The British Museum has the Tapling collection and others. There is a marvellous collection on free view to the public in the National Postal Museum at the General Post Office, St Martins-le-Grand, London E.C.1 The main part of the collection consists of stamps of Great Britain, presented by Reginald M. Phillips, and is almost complete from 1840 to the end of Queen Victoria's reign. Other collections in the National Postal Museum contain Commonwealth and foreign stamps from the Post Office records, and a visit to the museum is well worth while. Attractions there, besides the stamps on view, include film shows and lectures about Post Office activities.

Always remember that the more you learn about stamps the more interesting will your collection become. Although philately is such a vast subject that nobody could ever hope to know all there is to be known, it is only by adding to your knowledge continually that you will some day become an expert yourself.

# Index